My Black Job
A Story of Black Careers

Written and Edited by Cedric Strickland.
Illustrations by Cedric Strickland, using Adobe Creative Cloud and MidJourney.

© 2025 Cedric Strickland.
All rights reserved.

Published by Neua Publishing House, a division of Neua Holdings LLC.

Print ISBN   979-8-9925144-2-1
Ebook ISBN   979-8-9925144-3-8

THIS BOOK BELONGS TO:

_____

A Story of Black Careers

Preface

All around you, every day, people are doing amazing jobs all over the world.

In this book, we are going to explore many of these amazing jobs, from A to Z. As we explore, always remember, every job is a black job, and every job is something you can do too!

Now let's get started on our journey together, and discover many fun, new, and exciting careers.

Astronaut

The Space Traveler

Have you ever wanted to go to space? See the stars up close or walk on the moon? Sounds like you could be an astronaut!

Astronauts are highly trained scientists and engineers that travel to space to research alien worlds, perform experiments, and explore the cosmos.

Be an astronaut, it's out of this world!

Baker

The Pastry Artist

Do you love delicious treats, like yummy cakes and apple pies? Love the smell of freshly baked cookies? Sounds like you could be a baker!

Bakers are chefs that specialize in using ovens, science, and artistic flair to transform flour, sugar, and other ingredients into delicious, decadent delights.

Be a baker and make life a little sweeter!

Coder

The Tech Wiz

Do you love solving puzzles or building things? Ever wonder how the internet works or how voice assistants understand you? Sounds like you could be a coder!

Coders are software developers that design and build everything in the digital universe- from smartphone apps to video games, from alarm clocks to big screen animated films.

Be a coder and shape the future with technology!

Dancer

The Rhythm Rider

Can you move your body to a beat? Ever find a rhythm in your mind that gets you moving and grooving? Sounds like you could be a dancer!

Dancers are entertainers that use their bodies to tell stories, bring joy, inspire people, and create traditions through movements of flair and finesse.

Be a dancer, and let your body tell the story!

Entrepreneur

The Self Starter

Have a big idea? Ever think of something new and exciting that no one else has thought of? Sounds like you could be an entrepreneur!

Entrepreneurs are innovators who turn ideas into reality. They take risks, solve problems, and shape the future with their creativity and hard work.

Be an entrepreneur and build something great!

Farmer

The Grocery Grower

Love spending time outdoors? Enjoy growing plants or raising animals? Sounds like you could be a farmer!

Farmers grow crops, raise animals, and work hard to provide fresh fruits, vegetables, grains, and livestock needed to fill grocery stores and restaurants around the world.

Be a farmer and help feed the world!

Glassblower

The Lava Sculptor

Wonder how beautiful glass vases, sculptures, and decorations are made? Love creating things and being artistic? Sounds like you could be a glassblower!

Glassblowers use heat and skill to shape molten glass into amazing works of art and incredible, intricate sculptures; combining creativity and craftsmanship to make glass come to life.

Be a glassblower, and shape beauty from fire!

Handyman

The Toolbelt Titan

Are you good at fixing things? Enjoy taking things apart and putting them back together? Sounds like you could be a handyman!

Handymen are skilled workers who tackle all sorts of jobs using tools, creativity, and hands-on know-how to help people keep their homes and appliances in great shape.

Be a handyman and get hands-on!

Instructor

The People's Professor

Is it fun to help others learn new things? Love explaining ideas and watching people grow? Sounds like you could be an instructor!

Instructors teach new skills, share knowledge, and inspire students to reach their full potential in classrooms around the world and across the web.

Be an instructor and teach so many!

Jockey

The Modern Cowboy

Do you like cowboy movies? How about racing at full speed and crossing the finish line first? Sounds like you could be a jockey!

Jockeys are athletes that compete on horseback, riding horses in thrilling competitions. They train with skill, strategy, and courage to guide their powerful horses to victory on racetracks in front of thousands of fans.

Be a jockey and race toward greatness!

Karateka

The Dojo Master

Do action packed fighting scenes in movies catch your eye? Excited by throwing kicks and dodging punches? Sounds like you could be a karateka!

Karateka are martial artists that are skilled in karate, the action packed fighting style where you train hard, earn belts, and become masters of the craft.

Be a karateka and kick your way to the top!

Lawyer

The Justice Giant

Is it fun to debate with your friends and family? Do you enjoy solving problems and helping others? Sounds like you could be a lawyer!

Lawyers are professionals who help people solve problems by giving advice, creating contracts, or standing up to protect people's interests and rights.

Be a lawyer and use your knowledge to support others!

Marine

The All Star Defender

Imagine being a soldier that protects and defends? Do you dream of traveling the world? Sounds like you could be a Marine!

Marines are elite military professionals trained to defend and serve. They are skilled at teamwork, discipline, and have the strength to keep people safe.

Be a Marine and complete missions with your team around the globe!

Nurse

The Happy Healer

Do you enjoy helping others feel better? Does caring for people when they are sick interest you? Sounds like you could be a nurse!

Nurses take care of patients, and work alongside doctors to help people heal and stay healthy. They're often the heart of healthcare, offering kindness and expertise to those in need.

Be a nurse and put your healing hands to good use!

Oceanographer

The Water Scientist

Fascinated by water and the ocean's waves? Do you wonder about the secrets of the deep blue sea? Sounds like you could be an oceanographer!

Oceanographers explore the oceans; studying marine life, exploring underwater landscapes, and understanding the deepest depths of our big blue planet.

Be an oceanographer and dive into discovery!

Pilot

The Cloud Surfer

Dream of flying high? How about traveling the world and gliding on top of the clouds? Sounds like you could be a pilot!

Pilots are skilled aviators who navigate the skies, flying planes, jets, and helicopters to transport people and goods across cities, countries, and continents.

Be a pilot and take flight toward adventure!

Quarterback

The Playmaker

Love playing or watching sports? Ever wanted to be the one calling the plays and making big passes? Sounds like you could be a quarterback!

Quarterbacks are the strategists behind every play on the football field, guiding their teams' movements, making split second decisions, and delivering what it takes to win.

Be a quarterback and become greatness on the field!

Real Estate Agent

The Dream Maker

Always imagining your dream home? Do you imagine exploring and decorating homes of all shapes and sizes? Sounds like you could be a real estate agent!

Real estate agents tour homes, mansions, condos, and even boathouses across cities and suburbs, learning every style and design to help clients find the home of their dreams.

Be a real estate agent and change lives!

Social Media Influencer

The Digital Star

Do you love creating videos? Do you like sharing cool ideas or just making people laugh? Sounds like you could be a social media influencer!

Social media influencers connect with people worldwide. Making popular videos and creating interesting posts that bring their voice to the world.

Be a social media influencer, teach, entertain, and inspire every day!

Tailor

The Clothing Connoisseur

Have you ever been told that you are stylish? Do you enjoy imagining new ways to wear or design your clothes? Sounds like you could be a tailor!

Tailors are skilled at creating new looks from scratch by crafting unique designs, eye catching patterns, and well fitted clothing for clients and clothing brands.

Be a tailor and show off your style to everyone!

Urban Planner

The City Curator

Ever wonder how cities are built? Ever wanted to design communities or design better cities? Sounds like you could be an urban planner!

Urban planners create the layout of cities and towns, deciding the placement of parks, roads, and public spaces; designing in ways that make sure everyone is happy.

Be an urban planner, shape tomorrow's cities!

Violinist

The Music Magician

Do you love the sound of music? Ever dream of playing an instrument or performing on a stage? Sounds like you could be a violinist!

Violinists are musicians who create enchanting music in many styles, from classical symphonies to modern rap, violinists are on records, perform on stages, and even dazzle in movies.

Be a violinist and captivate all that listen!

Writer

The Pen Wielder

Ready to tell a story never heard? Ever dream of fantasy worlds and characters galore? Sounds like you could be a writer!

Writers use their imagination and skills to create stories, inform people, or entertain through words. Every movie, book, role playing game, and even every song has a writer behind the scenes to thank.

Be a writer, and let your words inspire hearts and minds!

Xtreme Sports Athlete

The Thrill Seeker

Love pushing physical limits, trying out daring stunts, and seeking thrills? Dream of doing the impossible? Sounds like you could be an Xtreme sports athlete!

Xtreme sports athletes perform adrenaline pumping events with finesse, technique, and courage, fearlessly competing in high-stakes competitions, and amazing audiences young and old.

Be an Xtreme sports athlete, become adventure!

Yacht Captain

The Wave Rider

Ready to go to sea and never look back? Do luxury boats and seaside destinations excite you? Sounds like you could be a yacht captain!

Yacht captains navigate oceans and seas, sailing the world to deliver majestic experiences and a safe journey for everyone on board.

Be a yacht captain and live life on the water!

Zoologist

The Animal Whisperer

Fascinated by animals and the wild? Could you see yourself studying nature up close and personal? Sounds like you could be a zoologist!

Zoologists are scientists who study animals, learning about their behaviors, and their habitats. Whether outside in nature, indoors in the lab, or at the zoo, zoologists research and protect the animal kingdom.

Be a zoologist and experience the wonders of the wild!

... and, the list goes on!

We Want To Hear From You

Did you know, anything you can imagine, you can achieve!

This book only tells part of the story, the rest of the story is with you.

It's never too early to imagine.
It's never too late to dream.

It's always the right time to share your passions with the world. We look forward to hearing from you, just use the hashtag #myblackjob!

About The Author

A Brief Biography

Cedric Strickland is the author, editor, and illustrator of the *My Black Job* book series, his passion for education, social justice, and technology inspire this series.

From Atlanta to Seattle. From Microsoft to Google. From University of Notre Dame student to University of Washington professor. From entrepreneur to author.

Cedric continues to break barriers on his journey of innovation, discovery, learning, and advocacy! Stay tuned for what's next!

www.ingramcontent.com/pod-product-compliance
Lightning Source LLC
Chambersburg PA
CBRC100102100526
44582CB00011B/168